A famous man once said, "A plain face is often surprisingly beautiful by reason of an inner light."

Likewise, plain days and dragging hours can come alive with beauty and splendor—if you know the secret.

We think you'll find the secret in this book.

*"Whatsoever things are true . . .
whatsoever things are lovely . . .
if there be any virtue, and if there be
any praise, think on these things."*

(Philippians 4:8)

Seven Splendid Moments

by Carmen Benson

*"Perhaps the unforgivable sin is
to have lived with something beautiful
and not have recognized it."*

— Author unknown

Whitaker House

504 LAUREL DRIVE, MONROEVILLE, PA 15146

To
DR. RAY CHARLES JARMAN

no friend on earth
is so dear to me as he

ISBN: 088368–054–8

WHITAKER HOUSE
504 Laurel Drive
Monroeville, Pennsylvania 15146
(412) 372-6420

FOREWORD

It was almost 30 years ago when I first met Carmen Benson . . .

She was then a nominal Bible believer. Since she was one of the Sunday School teachers in the church which I pastored, I tried to introduce her to the higher critical approach to the scriptures. This she strongly resisted.

When I began talking to her about the mental science teachings, she listened. Being an apt student, she soon far surpassed me in knowledge and understanding of these cults.

During this period, she became one of the secretaries of the church, with the responsibility of editing our weekly paper, which included editing my sermon summaries as well. Her writing ability was excellent, and she quickly won a position of high regard in the entire congregation. Her sharp and brilliant mind, combined with definite studious habits, took her deeper into the metaphysical cults, and these in turn took her farther away from the simple faith in God's Word which she originally had.

One night the Lord came to her in a dream and delivered her from this entanglement in false teachings and oriental philosophies. It completely transformed her life, and she became a dedicated Christian.

Immediately she immersed herself in the Bible and in devotional pursuits. After I found Christ myself, we co-authored a book, "The Grace and the Glory of God," published in 1968. Two years later her own masterly work, "Supernatural Dreams and Visions" was published. Since then, everywhere I go people ask me, "What was the dream Carmen Benson had that caused her to write this book?"

Now, for the first time, she tells it in "Seven Splendid Moments." The remarkable dream, and its interpretation, is related in full in one of the seven short stories in this book. In the scholarly presentation of her former writing, one recognizes a knowledgeable Bible student. But in this book, the reader becomes acquainted with the warm, friendly personality of the author herself.

Each of these narratives is a true account of a personal experience in her life, and is told in charming simplicity. These vignettes depict an array of splendid moments which include: an automobile accident on a snowy mountain; a mother's death at sunset; a daughter dressed in her wedding gown; a young army wife in a strange town during World War II; a letter to a grandaughter not yet

6

born; a supernatural dream with far-reaching consequences; and a coming home at last.

Some of the stories will bring a smile, and some a tear; but each brings a sweet breath of nostalgia, an intimate human touch with which everyone can identify. This little book is a gem, to be read and re-read and given to your best friends. One of the stories is particularly comforting to those who have lost a loved one, and another is especially enlightening to those who may be floundering around in spiritual doubt or uncertainty.

A woman sensitive to loveliness and to the things of the Lord, Carmen finds beauty in the everyday experiences of life—and she also finds God there. In these pages, you will find both delightfully revealed.

Dr. Ray Charles Jarman

January, 1974

CONTENTS

PREFACE

This is a collection of intimate and true
short stories, gathered together
as a spiritual bouquet
from the garden
of my life.

Now, looking back across the years, I see
how many times the Spirit of the Lord,
in tender loving kindness,
has given me beauty—
"beauty for ashes."

So often He used beauty and splendor—
in music, in nature, in words—
as a healing balm
for all kinds
of wounds.

Yes, God has blown a breath of loveliness
over the rough and ugly places,
the pain and the sadness,
the toil and
the tears.

May each one of these narratives be more
than just earthly experiences
with heavenly meanings
that happened
to me.

May they be something warm and personal,
a sweet fragrance of Christ,
something beautiful—
that happens
to you.

1974   *Carmen Benson*

MEDITATION AT TWILIGHT

~~~~~~

I stood at the window of my hospital room and looked out into the gathering darkness of early evening. Dusk—the loneliest, saddest time of day . . .

On the far horizon loomed a range of snow-covered mountains besprinkled with trees—the same majestic green pines and firs that rimmed the lake below. Snow, in large patches on the ground, extended up to the edge of the building. Not a person, not a car, not a house was visible anywhere.

The whole outside world was motionless and deserted, as silent as my private world inside a solitary room.

To the left a single lamp burned atop the corner of a projecting wing of the hospital. It illuminated the driveway leading to the ambulance entrance —the doorway through which I had been brought several days previously. Beneath me the light from my window was beginning to cast a pale golden reflection on the snow.

The endless afternoon had at last come to a

11

close. More long, empty hours stretched ahead until bedtime. There was nothing at all that I could do. I was unable to read, my eyes being slightly out of focus as a result of the injury to my head. There was no radio.

My roommate had left in the morning, and I felt her absence keenly. The doctor had already made his call. There would be no one else, for I was a long way from home.

Tomorrow I was to be released, and weeks of convalescence out of the hospital would commence. But tonight I was utterly alone in this remote place, separated from all that was familiar and dear.

How quickly and unexpectedly our lives can change! How drastically.

Sometimes it seemed that this must be a bad dream from which I would surely awaken—to find everything, including myself, "normal" again. At other times I was all too conscious that it was not a dream; and then various ugly fears regarding my injuries took possession of my mind. Perhaps I would never again be as I was before. They say no one ever completely gets over the effects of a brain concussion.

Manifold were the negative thoughts eager to occupy my attention. Deliberately I sought to replace them with more constructive thinking. I remembered the joyful invitation that had brought us from Los Angeles to Lake Arrowhead, high in the San Bernardino mountains . . .

"Can you and Jack drive up to Skyforest and enjoy a miracle with us?" our friend asked, her voice on the other end of the telephone bubbling with excitement.

"We always enjoy your beautiful mountain home," I told her. "But what is the miracle?"

"Last night there was a snowstorm, most unusual for the middle of April," she said. "This morning when we looked out, there was the miracle—bright sun shining on a world of sparkling beauty, glistening and white. The trees are like crystal lace against the blue of heaven, and there's magic in the air. Come up and stay overnight and behold all this loveliness!"

Hurriedly, my husband and I departed the city and drove to Skyforest. No sooner had we arrived, than our host and hostess took us for a sight-seeing excursion in their car. While en route to Running Springs, the snowstorm suddenly returned, and we were involved in an automobile accident.

The only one injured was I, and at first the injuries did not appear serious. I was able to go back to their mountain home and spend the night. However, by morning it was more than evident that I must be hospitalized.

As I recalled all of this, I brought to memory the glorious experience that had presented itself the morning following the accident . . .

We had been snowed in all night, but with daylight had come the snowplow, and then the ambulance. For the first time in my life I was to be carried on a stretcher.

One of the attendants covered me with blankets and wrapped a wool scarf around my head so that only my eyes were exposed. It was snowing lightly, and I had to be transported some distance from the house to the waiting vehicle.

Up the hill we started.

I ventured to take a look at the world from my unusual vantage point. Would that I had been a camera, for the breath-taking view I beheld was incredible—and obtainable only from this extraordinary perspective.

Above me, and all around, was a fairyland of fantastic beauty! I looked straight up into stately green pine trees, elegantly adorned with the pure white of newly fallen snow. Through a mist of delicate snowflakes, the artistry of branch and leaf was wondrously etched against a realm of softest white. It was sheer enchantment.

My anxieties vanished; my spirits became as exhilarated as the crisp, clean air.

We were going up a steep incline, and I could hear the labored breathing of those carrying me. I felt a tremendous wave of gratitude to them for so much exertion in my behalf. No matter how self-reliant we may like to think we are, there come times when we have great need of others.

The words: *"He shall give His angels charge over thee . . . They shall bear thee up in their hands . . ."* came to remembrance. That very

14

thing was literally happening to me now! Of course I knew perfectly well they were human hands, but how could angels bear you up in a physical world without physical hands? I was deeply impressed with a sense of kindness received . . .

"Do celestial beings really watch over us?" I wondered, as from the solitude of my hospital room I recalled this earlier experience.

"If they do, then where were you, my guardian angel, when that speeding truck came crashing into the rear of our car? . . . Where are you now? . . . Do you—does anyone—truly care for me? . . . Does God?"

The night had grown very dark, and still I remained at the window like some forlorn, earthbound ghost. There was no answer to my inquiries, no feeling that anyone heard; yet I kept asking questions of Someone, perhaps only of myself.

"Why must happiness be such an elusive visitor —a transitory guest in the human heart—while loneliness and difficulties so readily find lodgement? In fact, they never seem to depart.

"Are angels always happy? Do they," I pondered, "ever feel lonely or forsaken? . . . Or are they immune to the suffering, and disappointments, and sadness that we know?"

So many questions to add to all the others. Weren't there ever any answers?

In this trance-like state, suddenly I became aware of movement outside—the gentlest, loveliest kind of motion imaginable! Before my eyes there appeared three angelic forms gracefully ascending the path that curved around the hill on which my section of the building was located.

Against a backdrop of black velvet, these exquisite creatures with snow-white wings rhythmically glided between radiant spheres of golden light. Spellbound, I thought I had been privileged to catch a glimpse of some heavenly ballet in silent performance.

As they neared my window, the fascinating ballerinas could be more clearly distinguished. I recognized them as sisters from the religious order in charge of the hospital. Over their flowing white garments they wore long cloaks of white, which the brisk wind was causing to swirl about in winglike fashion.

I smiled to think that I had mistaken them for angels. And yet, how better to describe them—those whose entire lives were devoted to God and spent in caring for the sick and broken bodies of His children?

Just then one of the sisters turned her head toward the rectangle of light in which my figure was silhouetted, and for an instant her eyes contacted mine. A simple thing, inconsequential in itself. Merely a brief encounter of two of earth's mortals; yet I found myself profoundly moved, my heart strangely stirred.

There was no outward sign from either of us— no nod, or wave, or smile. There was, nevertheless,

16

a mysterious inner communication. It was as though two friendly hands had clasped, and a chord of understanding had somewhere sounded.

The loneliness that had been like a sickness immediately lifted. I no longer felt bereft of companionship—be it human or divine.

I still didn't know the whereabouts of my guardian angel—or whether or not I actually had one. Twice I had confused human beings with angels. First when they bore me up the mountain in their hands, and again when in the midst of terrible loneliness they passed before me in lovely array . . .

Could it be that now and then there really isn't much difference?

I didn't know the answers to any of my questions. But I did know there is a bond of kinship that unites those of us who love the Lord and want to serve Him—men, and angels, and sisters . . . and me. We all belong to the family of God. We all have need of each other. And many times we all are lonely, each in our own way.

Turning from the window, I looked above the door of my room at the image of Jesus, the crucified Christ, which hung there.

"Even You, upon occasion, felt alone and forsaken," I whispered. "And what we call 'happiness' did not always dwell with You. Neither was Your life without difficulty and anguish. Yet You proved that God does care . . . And I know He cares for me."

Comforted and gladdened in spirit, my mind full of remembered beauty, I pulled the draperies across the window for the night.

When I would again look out, it would be morning—the fairest, brightest part of day.

~~~~~~

*This is a factual account, just as it happened.
It is not embellished in any way whatsoever.
I have even reported the exact words spoken
(to the best of human recollection). It is my
prayerful wish that it may take a bit of the ap-
prehension and sadness out of that experience
we each must face sometime—with our loved
ones, and for ourselves.*

Mother was dying, I knew . . . It was June,
the month of her birth here on earth seventy-
seven years before. It would be the month of her
"rebirth" in heaven.

I stopped in to see her on my way home from
church. She was sitting in her familiar rocker, her
swollen legs propped up on the ottoman. A blanket
covered the pitiful little body that had for seven
years amazed the doctors by continuing to sustain
her courageous spirit, when medically that seemed
impossible. Her weary head rested on a faded blue
pillow.

Sitting down beside her, I took her hand. As I smoothed the hair from her forehead, I felt the silent pain of the knowledge that she was soon to leave the frail body to which she still clung, even yet.

Her eyes were closed, but I knew she was glad I was there. I told her what a beautiful sunshiny day it was, and asked if she could hear the birds singing. She said she could.

The bright summer day outside contrasted sharply with the wintry grayness inside—inside the house where death patiently waited, as reluctant to gather this brave little woman in his arms as she was to go with him . . .

"This day reminds me of a hymn I remember hearing you sing when I was a child, Mother— 'Beautiful Isle of Somewhere.' "

She had seemed asleep, but instantly she was alert and quickly recited the opening lines: "Somewhere the sun is shining; somewhere the songbirds dwell . . ."

I smiled, "Yes, dear. You remember too."

We sat without speaking for a time. These moments were precious, yet I didn't know how to use them or what to say. However, the next night I decided that it was a mistake to avoid the subject whose very presence was drawing more unavoidably near with every hour.

"Soon all this suffering will be over for you, Mother," I began; but I could sense she didn't

want to hear that. She was afraid of that vast unknown.

"Death is not our enemy, Mother. To a person
who is saved, and whose body is no longer able to
house the soul and spirit, death is a God-given
friend. Death, for those in Christ, comes as an
angel; did you know that? And the kingdom of
God is far lovelier than this."

She was silent. After a bit she said, "Earth life is
sweet."

"Yes, Mother, it is. But heaven is so much
sweeter."

I spoke of the wondrous beauties that awaited
her in the beyond, the fact that she would be re-
united with her loved ones there, and that she
would be freed from this worn-out, inadequate
body, which pained and humiliated her mentally
as well as physically.

She listened without comment until I made the
statement, "And you'll be young again, Mother."

"How do you know that?" she queried abruptly.

I was momentarily taken aback, but I answered
her as authoritatively as I could. She didn't seem
too convinced.

When it was time for me to go, I kissed her
goodnight, mindful that it might be the very last
goodnight of all. I was glad it was dark, so that
she could not see my eyes and their brimming
tears.

In final parting she said three words—with deliberate significance. They were these: "Always be happy."

The next night Mother was worse.

Laboriously, three of us together—my husband, my father, and I—struggled to get her from the bathroom to bed. Her body, which actually was emaciated, was so swollen with accumulated fluid that it was heavy and distorted beyond recognition.

She said Dad was hurting her by pulling her arms. She cried out, "Oh stop, stop, I can't go on!"

She would not move; and we couldn't move her. Then, without any warning, she collapsed. There was my mother—in that nightgown-clad, grossly misshapen body—fallen to her knees on the floor, calling out, "Oh God, help me!"

Somehow we got her to the couch, and she sank down, groaning with pain and panting from the exertion. I sat beside her, and with my arm around her tried to comfort her. I think I shall never again feel such utter and helpless misery.

"Compared to this," she gasped, "all my previous sufferings were a Sunday school picnic."

"It will soon be over, Mother, and all this will be forgotten. Just rest now. Everything is going to be all right." . . . She was the child now, and I the mother.

That night I prayed earnestly, "Dear God, please let her passing be easy. She has endured so much already. Let it be beautiful, and without pain. Lead her gently home, Father. Lead her gently . . . please . . ."

The next morning she was admitted to a convalescent hospital, and I visited her there several times. The doctor had given her sedation and she breathed heavily, her mouth agape.

In the room with her was another elderly woman who moaned and thrashed about continually. Her eyes were open and glassy. She was not a pretty sight . . . Truly, there is no sadness equal to the sadness of old age in its last sickness.

At one point during my afternoon vigil, Mother suddenly spoke so distinctly it seemed to be another voice issuing through her. The words were delivered in clear measured tones: "Changes must come . . . We each have our own destiny."

By Thursday, mucus was beginning to collect in her throat, and a faint noise could be detected in her breathing.

I asked a nurse to help me take off the ugly, harsh hospital gown, and instead we put on her prettiest flannel nightgown. It had a bit of ribbon and lace. I am glad we did that, for it was in that gown that she died.

When she roused, I talked to her about the goodness of God, and how beautiful was the experience that lay ahead of her. I asked her if she could see anything.

She said, "I see some children playing. They are calling out to me, 'You've got grass on top of your head!' "

23

The vision of the cemetery lot my father had recently purchased flashed in my mind's eye. I saw the green slope of Rose Hills, beneath whose sod her body would soon be placed.

I asked Mother if she could see anything else.

"I see animals, squirrels and farm animals. I don't see dogs, because I don't like dogs very much."

"Do you see any people?"

"Yes. I see my mother and my father."

The next day was Friday. When I came in the morning, Mother lay very still, but she was breathing. The noise in her throat was unmistakable now. She was ashen-faced, and appeared to be asleep.

The woman in the adjoining bed was coughing horribly, and groaning in loud agony. No one was with her. I had not seen anyone at any time come near her. Didn't anyone care about that poor wretched soul? I wondered. Her writhings increased, and her calls grew louder. Surely to the accompaniment of such nerve-racking sounds I would not have to say my final farewell to Mother!

Perhaps, however, I had already said it; and she to me. She no longer seemed to hear me. She looked very near the end. I waited a long time, but there was no change. She slept on.

When I returned with my father that afternoon, two startling alterations were immediately evident.

First, the other bed was empty. It was freshly made, its former tormented occupant gone . . .

mercifully. I realized that she must have died since I had been there shortly before noon.

All this registered only in the background of my mind. The real change was Mother . . . *She was transformed.*

She was sitting up, her eyes open, her face aglow! She, who had been in a coma, was now wide-awake and smiling. She seemed to have been eagerly waiting for us to arrive.

"I'm so happy!" she announced with all the excitement of a child on Christmas morning. "I'm so happy!"

My father and I were astonished; yet we found ourselves caught up in the spell of her radiant joy. It could be described in no other way. She was radiant; she was overflowing with joy. She *was* happy.

She smiled first at one of us, then the other. Turning to Dad she said, "I've *got* to go," and the way she said it conveyed the impression that she had already overstayed her time to the very limit.

Impulsively she touched the tip of his ear, much as a bride might do to her young husband. "You've been good to me," she said. And he who had cared for her all these many months, through wearisome days and exhausting sleepless nights, replied, "Not good enough, Mommy."

She turned to me, and her face was lighted from within. Her eyes sparkled with what she beheld that we could not see. "It's beautiful, beautiful,

25

beautiful!" She waved one arm expressively as though she were pointing out the heavenly vistas just above that surrounded us.

"And they're all here to welcome me!" she exclaimed rapturously.

"Are there angels, Mother?"

"Yes, there are angels." Her voice was a whisper now, but it held glory and wonder and contentment.

Then she said something we could not understand. We asked her to repeat it, but still we could not make it out. So she took her hand and ran it over her shoulders, and then in at her waist and over her hips, as one would outline a lovely youthful figure.

I knew what she was telling us . . .

Her old, distorted body was made new. The shoulders were no longer bony and caved-in; they were smooth and rounded. Her waist was slim again, her legs also. She was living proof of the realization of words written long ago:

"There is a natural body, and there is a spiritual body . . . And as we have borne the image of the earthy, we shall also bear the image of the heavenly.

"We shall not all sleep, but we shall all be changed, in a moment, in the twinkling of an eye . . ."

Mother continued to smile at us both. She was

happier than I ever remember seeing her—when it was living, not dying, that was at hand.

Imperative business demanded that I leave for about an hour; and so my father and I bade her goodbye, saying, "We will see you . . . again."

It was six-thirty in the evening before I returned alone. All the while I was away I kept repeating, "Wait for me, Mother. Please wait for me!" Now I dashed down the hall and into her room. Could she have lasted the hour I had been gone?

She was still there. Her eyes were closed, but she was breathing. Her mouth was open, as a sleeping baby's sometimes is. Bending close, I was aware of a strange odor coming from deep down inside her. It reminded me of ripe fruit that has fallen to the ground and lain there overlong.

Ever so gently I took her hand and spoke very quietly. "I came back, Mother. Not to hold you, dear. It's time for you to go, I know, and I would not hold you back. I prayed that you would wait for me, because I just wanted to be with you. But I am here now, and they are too . . . You go with them, dear . . ."

There was no change in either her peaceful expression or in the calm breathing. I kept hold of her hand and waited beside the bed. Outside the sounds of the moving world went on in the distance.

It was almost seven o'clock, a brief fifteen minutes before what was to be her last breath, when I did an involuntary thing . . .

Without aforethought, and almost in an experimental nature, I said aloud, but very softly, "Mother, if you can hear me, could you . . . smile at me . . . as you did this afternoon?"

Before I had quite finished my sentence, her mouth instantly turned up in a bright and definite smile. Unmistakable, unimagined—unforgettable.

"Oh you sweet Mother! Even now you grant my request."

My brother came in shortly afterward, as did our minister. And so it was that the three of us were there with her when she gently departed from our midst. We watched her tranquil breathing become more shallow, and the breaths grow farther and still farther apart, and finally cease altogether.

Yet even after that, a faint pulse beat in her throat. Her faithful heart—which had withstood two severe attacks of coronary thrombosis, and a later intestinal operation—had not given up until she had freely chosen to leave it behind. It served her well, to the very end.

The doctor came to make the routine examination. At the door just before he left, he glanced a last time at the motionless body on the bed and remarked, "She's in peace now."

"No, doctor," I said to myself, "it's better than that. She's in paradise."

The next day I was walking down the street, thinking about Mother, when a sudden and vivid realization impressed itself strongly upon my mind. It was almost as if I heard her say to me, "I'm younger now than you are!"

Despite my surprise at the very thought, I had to smile. I remembered the night I had told her, "Mother, you'll be young again," and she had found it hard to believe. Now both of us *knew* that not only was she young, but younger than I!

On Sunday all our family went to church together. So many Sundays Mother had crept feebly down the aisle to sit like a wounded bird in the seat next to mine. Today I "saw" her walking with gaiety and lightness. What though it was in the invisible? In Christ, she was with us still.

At the funeral, her sacred ceremony of final parting from us for awhile, the organ began the soft sweet notes of "*Somewhere the sun is shining . . . somewhere the songbirds dwell . . .*" Indeed there was in our hearts no "sad repining," for we knew that "God lives, and all is well . . .

> "*Somewhere, somewhere,*
> *Beautiful isle of somewhere!*
> *Land of the true, where we live anew,*
> *Beautiful isle of somewhere.*"

Later at the cemetery where her earthly graduation service was completed, the pink flower-bedecked casket was set down on the grass, ready for lowering into the warm brown earth. I remembered the children she had seen playing, and how

29

they had called out, "You've got grass on top of your head!"

It hadn't troubled her then; it did not trouble her now. It was simply a happy way of picturing a happy event. For Mother had gone to be with her Lord; and though we felt our loss, we rejoiced for her gain.

We knew that the death of her physical body was only her soul changing clothes . . . setting aside the heavy and cumbersome outer garment, that she might put on the luminous robes of glory.

For her, it was sunrise; and all the birds of heaven were singing.

THE WEDDING GOWN

～～～～～～～～～～～～～～～～～～～～～～～

S tanding in front of the three-way mirror in the department store dressing room, the young woman surveyed herself as a bride.

In a chair beside her sat the mother, who quietly watched as the crown of pearls and sparkling brilliants was placed atop her daughter's blond head—and the silk illusion veil adjusted to fall over her face, as it would for the actual ceremony.

The French saleslady was right; this gown was perfect. "Oh you are so petite!" she had exclaimed. "I know just the dress for you!" And among all the others, it alone was apparently fashioned especially for her.

She looked like a fairy princess, and Cinderella-at-the-ball, and an angel from heaven—all merged into one shining, lovely creature.

"Ever since I was a little girl, I've looked forward to the day when I would be a bride," the young woman happily confided to the saleslady. Then, turning around slowly to examine every view, she said, "Well, Mother, how does it seem to see your daughter dressed in her wedding gown?"

How does it seem . . . ?

For a moment the question evoked a strange ache—half sweet, half sad—in the mother's throat. In her heart was the poignant realization that this marked a major change along life's ever-changing way.

The mother was a long time in answering.

How does it seem to see your daughter dressed in her wedding gown? To look through a misty veil at the radiant face of a nineteen-year-old, and to see instead another face . . . a whole series of faces . . . yet all of them that same dear face you first glimpsed inside a pink blanket in a hospital room . . .

"Here she is," the nurse had said as she presented her little bundle to the anxiously waiting young mother. "We call her 'The Peanut' in the nursery because she's so small."

How precious was that first beholding! It seemed too good to be true. Your baby was alive, and perfectly equipped with the correct number of fingers and toes and eyes and ears . . . Oh thank You, God, for giving her to me! Thank You, thank You!

During the days and weeks and months that followed, there were many wonderful changes to observe. The fringe of dark hair turned out to be blond and naturally curly, just as you had hoped it would. The eyes were blue, and they looked at you with such purity and innocence. That first sweet smile; the first sign of a tooth; the day she laughed aloud for the very first time . . .

Sometimes the changes were frightening to an inexperienced and nervous young mother. A sudden high fever; a choking in the throat; dark shadows under eyes that were weary from the ravages of another bronchial asthma attack; red spots— were they chicken pox or measles or something even worse . . . ?

Yet the bad times always changed too, eventually. Even as health had become sickness, so sickness yielded to recovery.

All at once it was her first day at kindergarten. And with it began the severing of the ties of dependency. Baby days were forever past. Now the partings would ensue.

As for the child, she had eagerly looked forward to that important day, the day when she would at last be a "schoolgirl." It wasn't long before she was walking all the way home alone. Mother would stand on the sidewalk, her eyes straining at the horizon to catch sight of that little figure as it rounded the corner . . .

Childhood's tender years, so quickly gone. Toys and tricycles, finger paints and roller skates, Halloween costumes and Christmas presents, stuffed animals and dolls. So many dolls; yet of their number, one was treasured above all the rest.

This was that glorified personage who represented everything beautiful and thrilling to a little girl—the captivating and glamorous Bride Doll!

The doll made her initial appearance several weeks before a coming church bazaar. The mother was making the white satin bridal gown which she would wear, complete with tiara and veil and bouquet. In addition to this she was to possess an entire trousseau of clothes.

Sewing went on for days, and all the while the child watched the fascinating proceedings she kept saying, "Oh Mother, I know I'm going to be the one who gets the Bride Doll in the drawing! I've been praying every night for her."

"Better wait and see, dear. Lots of other little girls are probably praying for her too. But since she can only be given to one, you mustn't be too disappointed if you aren't the lucky one."

At last the long-awaited day of the bazaar arrived, and the Bride Doll was displayed in all her splendor in the booth at which she was the featured attraction. Gathered around her were many little girls, all gazing up at her with bright shining eyes. They could hardly wait for the drawing to take place.

"I want her so much, Mother," whispered the child. "She's the most beautiful doll I've ever seen, and I want to hold her and have her always as my very own."

"Remember what Mother said about not being too disappointed . . ."

There was a tension-packed moment as the tickets were stirred, followed by a breathless hush just before the name was selected. Then came the announcement. And after that glad squeals of delight from one little girl, and sighs and tears from all the others.

The supremely favored one who took home in her welcoming arms the much-coveted prize . . . was *not* the child.

Later, at bedtime, she sobbed, "She was mine. I watched her every day, and I loved her so. Now she belongs to someone else!"

It was a time when great consolation was needed. The mother spoke comfortingly, "But little one, you had the joy of all those days of seeing her become the Bride Doll." She gathered her daughter close in her arms, kissing the tear-drenched face. "And even though you love her still, now someone else will love her too."

Nevertheless the child cried herself to sleep that night. The muffled sounds of her grief at the irretrievable loss mingled in the house with the hum of a sewing machine in the next room.

Despite the fact that during the next few weeks Mother's room frequently became "Santa's Workshop"—and at these times the child was honorbound not to go in, not even to peek—come Christmas morning, she simply could not understand the miracle that occurred.

For there, nestled in the first package she opened, was the beautiful Bride Doll herself! Somehow she looked even more splendid than she had at the bazaar. And in several of the other boxes were exact duplicates of her entire trousseau!

35

Oh the overwhelming joy of it! . . . Life has its moments of ecstatic happiness, its wondrous ways of reassuring us that God has not forgotten after all.

Now there stood before the mirror in a department store a living Bride Doll—this one not made with hands; but like the other, dearly cherished and treasured.

It seemed incredible that so many years could have come and gone so quickly. One day the child was in grammar school, and the next in Junior High . . . And then she was going out on her first date . . .

Such excitement. A new dress, a little bit of Mother's perfume, and a considerable bit of her advice. They were going to the movies, but since the boy was not old enough to drive, his father had to take them and bring them home (performing his role as inconspicuously as possible, of course).

The girl's father decided he would go along to keep the other man company. In fact, they might as well take in the show as long as they were at it. In the theater the fathers were careful to sit some distance in back of the young pair, thoroughly certain that their presence was no hindrance.

Yet, to the girl, the evening didn't prove to be quite as romantic as she had expected. But then, seldom is life able to measure up to our dreams.

Other reflections drifted through the mother's memory . . .

An afternoon in June, and the girl in white cap and gown walking up to receive her high school diploma. How proud her parents were to hear the words: "Graduated with honors."

College days followed, and with them the full realization that the girl was now an adult with a life all her own.

One experience always gives way to another. Last summer marked the engagement party, and this summer would be the wedding. The young woman was as eager to launch out on her married life as she had been, as a child, to begin her school days.

At the present moment she was busy studying the embroidery detail on the sleeve of the bridal gown.

"You haven't answered my question, Mother," she remarked.

How does it seem to see your daughter dressed in her wedding gown . . . ?

In her heart the mother was thinking, "It seems as though part of my life is ending . . . and gone . . . a lovely part that can never come again.

"She's so young—just a child. And yet she is almost two years older than I was when I became a bride. Perhaps my mother felt about me then as I do now . . . My mother, who never lived to see this day . . . Will I, too, be gone when the child of my child reaches the marriage age . . . ?

"How brief is the span of our days . . . When we are young, the road of life appears endless,

37

continually beckoning us onward. So much awaits ahead. And then we reach a few turns—and the knowledge that the road is much shorter than we thought. Already more of it stretches in back of us than is left ahead . . . Indeed, it is not endless."

But these are scarcely things you say to one who stands on the brink of such a felicitous beginning.

The moments passed, and at last the mother began to voice an answer.

"Darling, do you remember the night of the church bazaar a long time ago when you were a little girl? It was the time you had to face the fact that you couldn't keep the Bride Doll you so dearly loved."

The daughter smiled. "Yes, I remember."

"You said then, 'She was mine, and I loved her so! Now she belongs to someone else.'" The mother paused, then added softly, "I feel a little like that now."

The younger woman looked at her mother with pensive understanding. "I'll never forget how I cried, and you tried to comfort me."

"Well, dear, I won't cry," said the older woman reassuringly. "But if ever I need to be comforted, I think God will tell me the same thing I told you then. He will remind me that I had the joy of all those years watching you become a beautiful bride . . . You see, dear, nothing on this earth— no matter how cherished—can be retained. We can only keep the joy of it. If we are thankful to God for the blessings and the privilege of the experience, we shall never really lose it."

The daughter stood very still, thinking over what her mother had said. For an instant she had the strange impression that the past, the present, and the future were all interrelated fragments of one picture.

The mother went on, "I also recall saying to you that night that although you still loved the Bride Doll, someone else will love her too . . . Now, it's my turn to accept the truth of those words . . . and to relinquish my little doll."

For a fleeting moment, like an echo from the past, came to mind the sound of a sewing machine in another room. Its hum, as on that other night, carried a hint of promise, seeming to foretell of blessings yet to be.

And with the remembrance, the mother felt her sadness dissolve. In its place there rose a quiet inner joy.

She said to her daughter, "Life is full of changes; inevitably they come our way. Some of them hurt a little, and occasionally bring tears. But life also has its Christmas mornings, its miraculous surprises. For in back of everything is the plan of a Loving Heavenly Parent who cares for His own.

"That's the reason," concluded the mother, "that in God's good time, I think we are going to find another Bride Doll. Only this one will arrive, not

39

with a trousseau, but with something even nicer . . . a layette!"

The two of them, the bride and the mother-of-the-bride, laughed happily together.

It was time for the fitting of the wedding gown.

HE SHALL DIRECT THY PATHS

The year was 1943 . . . It was springtime, and World War II was blazing its trail of fiery destruction and bloodshed over most of the earth. Total war had altered the affairs of every person, every home, every city—and many lives had been torn up by the roots.

Mine was one of them.

Due to its proximity to a large army training camp, the little town of Medford, Oregon was overrun with people. Army wives by the hundreds had flocked into the area seeking to follow husbands who had been sent to Camp White.

The effects of rationing were much in evidence —food and gasoline preeminently. Long lines of customers waited to gain entrance to restaurants, along with the town's few places of entertainment. Both proffered inferior fare; but with nothing else available, there was even a scarcity of complainers.

Particularly was there a shortage of housing.

The demand for living quarters, even of the most humble kind, far exceeded the supply. Hotels, motels, apartments were jammed; and each had extensive waiting lists. Some private homes opened up rooms for rent, but all accommodations were insufficient to take care of the swarming influx. Many a person spent the night in a smelly, noisy, overcrowded bus or railroad station.

It was the dismal hour of five o'clock in the morning when I arrived in Medford, another of the many army wives to step from the Greyhound bus into the depot's bleak surroundings.

There was no one to meet me; but I was accompanied by a girl named Betty, whose husband had also recently been inducted into the service. We had made the trip from Los Angeles together.

In the beginning of our journey, we shared a mutual spirit of gay adventure—though we had little else in common. She was an ultra-sophisticate and found my interests rather boring, especially my conversation about the church. Despite the fact that we were only in our early twenties, we were thoroughly exhausted by the time we alighted from that bus.

Indeed, we had good reason to be . . .

At Martinez where we changed trains, we had found ourselves on one of the most dilapidated, ancient vehicles ever encountered outside a museum. It was restored to service only because of the tremendous amount of travel that war always entails. Our seats had been taken by a group of military personnel, who had undisputed priority over civilians.

In the stuffy railroad car where we were assigned, it was almost impossible to breathe. We sought escape in the ladies' lounge; but this was even worse, for it offered neither air nor running water! And no attempt was made to correct its increasingly offensive condition.

We finally found a tiny open-air section, a kind of connecting link between cars. Wrapping our coats tightly around us for warmth, we stood up all the way from Martinez to Dunsmuir (where we were to transfer to a bus)—a trip which took most of the night . . .

Now we had at last reached our destination.

We hastened to the Hotel Jackson, where we had telegraphed in advance for reservations. Here we were in for a jolt of another kind. The desk clerk confirmed our reservations, but with the notation that we were twenty-fifth and twenty-sixth on the waiting list! It might be two or three days before rooms would be available.

All our protests and pleadings were met with a repeated: "I'm sorry. There's nothing I can do about it."

Stunned, sleepy, and tired, we dropped our suitcases at our feet and sank into a nearby sofa. We tried to think what to do. Betty went to a phone booth and called the other hotels, but we couldn't even get on a waiting list anywhere else. We resumed our places on the sofa.

The lobby was crowded with an assortment of

43

other "refugees." We were luckier than many of them who couldn't find a place to sit down.

Closing our eyes, we lay our heads back and tried to go to sleep. But worry over our plight kept prodding at our minds. I breathed a few silent, desperate prayers; but I couldn't imagine how even God could help under these circumstances.

I don't remember how long we were there before the desk clerk approached us.

"We have a room that has just been vacated," he said. "It is a double room, meant for four people, and the price is twice that of a regular room. But since you two are friends, perhaps you would want to take it."

Sharing a room with another couple didn't provide the ideal setting for a reunion with our husbands; but needless to say, we lost no time in accepting occupancy. The room would certainly do until we could find separate quarters someplace else.

This, however, did not prove an easy task.

Day after day we spent our time haunting real estate offices, and trekking from store to store in the business district applying for work. Every establishment was thronged with army wives desirous of obtaining employment.

Betty had held an excellent position in one of Los Angeles' most fashionable department stores, and she was hired by the best dress shop in town. I was unsuccessful even in the ten cent stores.

44

To add to her good fortune, on the same day she landed the job, her husband phoned to say that he had located a room for her through one of the departing soldiers on the post.

Happily, she began to pack her things. She had made a quick recovery from the flu which had stricken her a few days after our arrival. I was just coming down with it.

"I hate to leave you like this," she told me as she said goodbye; but it was difficult to discern the slightest trace of regret in either face or voice.

Be that as it may, I couldn't blame her. My troubles were not hers, and her more favored lot merited rejoicing . . . On her part, at least.

She did offer to leave me some cold tablets for the flu, which she had also bestowed upon me.

Ill, and alone, and frightened—I took stock of my predicament. I could not stay in this expensive room much longer. Paying half the rent had been bad enough, but the full amount was prohibitive—especially with no job. I would have to find a room somewhere—anywhere.

Gulping down some of the pills, I got dressed and started out—determined to walk all over Medford, if necessary, until I found a room. I was attired in my best suit, and wearing high heels; for I thought an attractive appearance might aid my chances.

I made the rounds of all the real estate offices, inquired at the U.S.O. and the Red Cross; but came up with only one possibility. The agent said it was a little distance at the outskirts of town, and there was no phone; but I grabbed the address, and walked hurriedly down the streets he had specified. I hoped the room would not be gone before I got there.

The high heels and my perspiring reaction to the flu and the pills were beginning to take their toll.

I walked for blocks—miles it seemed. The district became shabbier and shabbier. Abruptly the pavement turned into a dirt road, and the sidewalks ended. It was evident I could pursue this no further.

Sick at heart as well as in body, I retraced my steps toward town, growing more dejected by the moment. My mind began to fill with bitterness. Why didn't God help me?

I thought of our friends at home who had not even been drafted. Many of them were in defense plants making more money than they ever had in their lives; while we had been forced to abandon our apartment and our small business (there was no time to sell it).

Jack was a buck private in the infantry, and we had only the prospect of a few months together before he would be shipped overseas—no doubt to the front lines, possibly to be wounded or killed. Here I was hundreds of miles from where I belonged, a stranger in a strange land. I pictured my flu getting worse and turning into double pneumonia . . .

46

From a spiritual standpoint it seemd particularly unfair to me that God would let Betty—who never went to church, was completely indifferent to religion—acquire a room and a good job, and leave me with nothing but the flu she had given me!

I kept wallowing in self-pity, and mumbling recriminations against the injustices of life.

But by the time I reached the central area again, my mental and emotional resentment had burned itself out. (Not so the physical burning in my feet.) My negativity had passed; nevertheless, I felt utterly defeated in spirit. I would have to give up and return to Los Angeles.

"Oh dear God," I whispered imploringly, "won't You please help me? I have no one but You!"

At this point of letting go, a strange kind of tranquility came over me. I yielded myself to its peace . . .

I was crossing a side street, and walking very slowly, when suddenly I received the most extraordinary impression. It came as clearly as if a voice behind me had spoken:

"Turn to the right."

For a moment I paused, somewhat perplexed. I must be hearing things. But since that street led in the general direction of the hotel, I shrugged my weary shoulders and obeyed the mysterious command.

In the middle of the block, the voice came a

second time. Very plainly and distinctly I heard the words:

"*Turn to the left.*"

This time I thought someone surely must have spoken alóud. I glanced all around, but no one was in my immediate vicinity. I looked at the surroundings. It was a street on which I had never been. I had passed a large market on the corner, and the only thing on my left was the building next to it, which was set back on the lot. A sign in front designated it as an Elks Lodge.

I hesitated. The voice repeated its instructions: "*Turn to the left. Go into that building.*"

Nothing like this had ever happened to me before. Was I in a daze of some kind? Perhaps those pills . . . How could I possibly find a room to rent in an Elks Hall?

Yet I found myself going up the walk, trying the door. It was unlocked, and it opened at my touch. Inside there was a hallway leading into a larger assembly room. No one was in sight, though I had the strange feeling that I was not alone.

Just then a woman came in the front door and walked toward a desk in the corner of the room. Seeing me, she smiled and asked if she could be of any help.

"Yes," I murmured, as though I were reciting a line from a play. "Do you know of any place where I might rent a room?"

At once she exclaimed in an attitude of pleasant surprise, "Why, yes I do! I was just in the market next door and ran into a friend of mine who has been renting out a room in her home. Her husband is overseas with the Merchant Marine. The girl who has been staying there has to leave very suddenly—tonight, in fact—and my friend asked me if I knew of someone who would like to have the room."

My heart leaped within me! Before I could reply, the woman continued. "Mrs. Hansen is very particular, however. She won't take anyone who smokes or drinks."

"Neither my husband nor I smoke or drink," I hastened to declare.

"Also, she is a devout Lutheran and prefers a church person."

"We are lifelong church people. My husband is a deacon in the Wilshire Christian Church in Los Angeles, California."

This was sufficient assurance. The woman said, "You wait here. I'll go back to the market, and if she is still there, I'll bring her in and she can interview you herself. But I think you are just what she is looking for!"

While she was gone, I prayed with all my strength that I would be acceptable, and that the room would be decent and not too expensive.

As things turned out, I and the room and the price were all very acceptable.

Mrs. Hansen was a warmhearted, cheerful and kind person; and her home proved to be everything home should be. It was in a quiet residential district where the lush greenery of Oregon the Beautiful abounded. Azaleas and rhododendrons flourished in profuse splendor around the white frame dwelling.

My room-to-be was comfortable and attractive; and just outside the window, a flowering quince tree in all its pink perfection was in full bloom.

When we had concluded our arrangements, Mrs. Hansen offered to take me back to the hotel, and said she would call for me the next morning. To use precious gasoline on my behalf was an added measure of graciousness. I was about to burst asunder with gratitude to her and to God.

Somewhere along the line, even the flu took its leave. I was too busy to note its exact departure . . .

Yes, the table God prepares for us is an abundant one. This was further demonstrated when Mrs. Hansen invited me to have dinner with the family—a teenage daughter, and a small son. Her cooking was superb, and my appreciation so boundless that she granted me the privilege of board, as well as room, for a very modest amount. She said Jack was welcome to join us whenever he could get in from camp.

Thus it was that a few evenings later all of us were sitting in the living room enjoying delightful music, having just finished another of Mrs. Hansen's culinary feasts. She was at the piano, and her daughter played the accordion.

50

Jack commented to me, "This is some contrast to Betty's situation! I learned from her husband today that she is very unhappy. Her room is little more than a dingy hole in some ramshackle house, so near the river that mosquitos constantly plague them. The place has no living room, or kitchen privileges. She has to eat all her meals out, and you know what these restaurants are like."

I recalled with shame my resentment toward God for seemingly being partial to Betty and neglectful of me.

Our heavenly Father *does* hear the prayerful cry of our hearts. He does answer our needs. Sometimes we have to wait a little for Him to arrange the details. It took a bit of maneuvering to bring Mrs. Hansen and me together in the same place at just the right time. Yet so clearly did He guide my footsteps, and so generously did His answer come.

In the more than thirty years which have since elapsed, I have often remembered the lesson this experience taught me . . .

Troubles may appear overwhelming; but when we cease our negative attitudes toward them, and quit rushing around in our own frantic way— when we earnestly seek the help of God in prayer, and trustingly yield ourselves to Him—a state of inner calm will follow. Then His loving care and tender guidance can get through.

I do not know whether it was the voice of an angel, or the voice of the Holy Spirit Himself, who directed my path that day. Certainly, it was no accidental happenstance, no figment of the imagination.

Truly the Bible tells us:

"He will be gracious to you at the sound of your cry. When he hears it, he will answer you. And though the Lord give you the bread of adversity and the water of affliction, yet your Teacher will not hide himself any more . . .

"And your ears shall hear a word behind you saying, 'This is the way, walk in it,' when you turn to the right, or when you turn to the left.'" (Isaiah 30:19–21 RSV)

"Trust in the Lord with all thy heart, and lean not on thine own understanding. In all thy ways acknowledge him, and he shall direct thy paths." (Proverbs 3:5,6)

LAST NIGHT I HAD A DREAM . . .

Godspoke to me through a dream—months before I really knew Him.

No ordinary dream was this . . . Perhaps it should be called a vision—an inner vision seen as a dream. Whatever you call it, it was for me the key that finally unlocked life's greatest secret.

So unusual was its content, so symbolical its presentation, so complex, yet so smooth its sequence that it was unlike anything I have ever known before or since. And when it had unfolded, I was awakened immediately—stabbed awake with the impact of it.

For a few moments I lay in the pre-dawn stillness recalling every vivid detail. Its meaning surpassed my comprehension.

I found myself getting up and writing it down. The dream seemed more real than the paper and pencil I was using to record it, the table on which I was writing, or the visible familiar world around me. It seemed more real than my own self.

I was aware that it had been impressed upon

my mind by a higher Being—a greater, wiser Self than mine . . . But why? What was it trying to tell me? What was its revelation?

For days, weeks, and months I sought to decipher its significance, to ferret out its message. In prayer I asked God to divulge its secret. His only answer was, "You must learn that for yourself, my child."

"Then please help me," I implored.

Assuringly came the reply, "I will."

A thorough ransacking of my own mind, and of literature on the subject, resulted in a maze of ideas and possibilities. But none of these interpretations of the parts fit together with the whole of the dream. Neither did they carry that intuitive weight of authority that convinces one, "This is the truth."

As a last resort, I foolishly invoked the aid of a woman who had written a book on dream interpretations. But in her attempt to explain the dream, she proved to be as ineffective as were the soothsayers, astrologers, magicians, and sorcerers of Biblical times.

"The same symbols have varied meanings," she informed me, "and to interpret a dream properly can be very exacting."

"Well, God," I remarked after hearing this, "I have learned nothing about the dream You gave me, except that all my efforts to interpret it have turned out to be futile. You will have to reveal its meaning to me in Your own way. I only hope I will recognize it when it comes."

"When the answer is given," said the Lord, "you will know it."

God's ways of teaching can be very unpredictable. His ways are not our ways. But finally the last piece of the puzzle came forth, and I knew for a certainty the full meaning.

I tell it now to you—this strange dream—just as I recorded it that morning . . .

I was part of a milling crowd of people in a common street scene. From above there appeared a small, white bird—pure white—flying down. This most unusual bird was encircled by a ring of light, atop which were little lighted prongs, like candles on a crown. The lights were living, burning bits of flame.

The bird was not afraid of people. It flew down and hovered over my right shoulder. Was it going to light there? No. It settled on the top of my head, slightly toward the back!

It didn't go away. It just stayed there, its lights brightly sparkling.

I expected people to see it and think, "How strange!" for the wonder of the bird itself fascinated me, and the fact that it was resting on top of my head was even more of a wonder. But as I walked along the busy thoroughfare, only one or two paid any notice.

Continuing on my way, my thoughts and feelings were mixed. I felt rather happy about this phenomenon, though somewhat mystified.

As I passed store fronts, I tried to catch my reflection in their windows, but I couldn't see much. The lights around the bird began to flicker and grow dim. Some went out. But I could still feel the activity of the living bird on my head.

Once I wondered if it might be making a nest in which to give birth to its young, but that thought was too much for me to be comfortable about. After all, this was taking place on top of my head! Then I wondered if the bird's bill might peck my scalp, but my hair seemed adequate protection.

After awhile the fluttering lessened, and all was completely still. Then I realized I must get this off my head.

Reaching upward, I encountered bands of cloth swathing the bird. When I finally pulled them all off, the bird lay in the center—*dead*. I could see its dead face and body so plainly. The bedraggled feathers didn't look as white as before. The ring and the lights were not in evidence.

The real sight was the quantity of blood that had soaked from the bird and stained the white material with huge streaks of crimson!

"How could that little bird have had all that blood?" I marveled.

Wrapping the whole bundle carefully around

my right hand, much like a large muff, I sought someplace to put it down and to check my head; for I felt it must be matted with the same blood. What a mess that would be! I would have to get some water and wipe off my hair before the blood dried and caked on it.

I came to a big, impressive church and went up the steps. The several front doors were open and people were entering. But when I came into the large foyer, there were turnstiles in the center, and money was being taken at each one. A Christmas pageant was going on inside the sanctuary behind velvet-draperied doors. I could hear the music and the singing.

An attendant—a young man dressed in a very fancy usher's costume—quickly approached me, and seeing the swathe of blood-stained material around my hand said, "You can't come in here with that!"

"I don't want to see the performance," I told him. "I just want to put this somewhere and fix my hair."

He refused me admission.

Then, in a slightly angry, authoritative way, I informed him that I was in the employ of the church.

He was immediately taken aback and said, "Oh, excuse me."

I strode along to my right in the large foyer, wondering why people didn't take me for an accident victim. No one seemed to pay the least attention. I found a large, almost empty receptacle to the side of one of the turnstiles, and put the bundle in it.

Then I walked back to the left of the foyer.

Along one wall in the corner were two doors of highly polished wood. I hoped one would lead to a place where I could repair myself. On both doors were markings—symbols and numbers—but on the farthest one I made out the gold letters "WOTAN." I entered.

Inside was a kind of anteroom. There was water available—even the glass shelves were wet with water. There was a large mirror, but I had no hand mirror to examine the top of my head. A kindly woman was there, and she offered to assist me.

There the dream ended.

For several weeks I was haunted by the dream and frustrated by my inability to obtain an interpretation. What did that bird symbolize? Why did the lights flicker and go out; and where did all those swathings of cloth wrapped around my head come from?

Most important of all, why did the bird die? The blood no doubt denoted suffering, but it could not be my suffering, for it was not my blood. The death of the bird continued to trouble me. And all that blood. What did it really mean? I thought about it, prayed and meditated; but no solution was forthcoming.

One morning some weeks later, I received the answer, and from a most unexpected source . . .

I was alone in the house, and decided to turn on the radio. The station to which it was already tuned was just playing the closing bars of a hymn. A man's voice began to speak:

"A minister was trying to teach a farmer about the meaning of Christ's death on the cross, but all of his theological dissertations fell on deaf ears. One day he paid a visit to the farm.

" 'Come on out here,' called the farmer. 'I want to show you something.' And he led the minister to the chicken yard. There, sitting perfectly still on her nest, was a mother hen. 'Touch her,' the farmer said.

"The minister did so, and was shocked to discover that the hen was cold and stiff. She was dead.

" 'A weasel came in the night and killed her,' explained the farmer. 'Sucked the blood out through her head. She didn't run away—died to save the little chicks that were under her wings. She sacrificed her life for them! Isn't that something?'

" 'It certainly is,' responded the minister. 'And it is exactly what Jesus did for you on Calvary . . . Now do you understand, my friend?' "

Listening to this, I almost dropped the dish I was washing—not because of the story, but because of its similarity to my dream. I turned off the radio and stood motionless beside it.

Could it be that the pure white bird in my dream signified Jesus Christ? If so, that would explain its death. Was this the key to the entire interpretation?

Like the chickens, I had been under the bird's wings. And it had not left me, but had died—and its blood had drenched all that material covering my head. Those swathings had not come from the bird, but from me. Did they represent the accumulation of matter that was wrapped around me —thoughts, beliefs, failings, imperfections, fears, guilts and mistakes . . . ? Sins, in other words.

If so, the cloths should have been black. Or red, at least. But they were white . . .

Was it possible that the blood had made them so?

I remembered that the Bible speaks of the robes of the multitude that were washed and made white in the blood of the Lamb. And I recalled another scripture: *"Though your sins be as scarlet, they shall be as white as snow; though they be red like crimson, they shall be as wool."*

Tears started to sting my eyes. I went to my place of prayer and knelt down, hands clasped, face upturned. As simply as a child, I asked God to please let me speak directly to Jesus.

Instantly He was there! Never before had I felt such a blessed Presence.

Very haltingly, I whispered: "Dear Lord Jesus . . . Was the pure white bird in my dream—You?

Was its dead body—Your body, broken—for me?
Was its blood—Your blood, poured out—for me?
Did You make all my unworthiness—all my un-
righteousness—clean and white? Did You do that
—for me . . . ?"

Then I added one more question.

Because, up to this point I regarded Him only
as the impersonal Saviour of the world, I had to
know if He really could be a personal Saviour. Did
He really die for me as a specific individual, not
merely as one of the billions in the mass of man-
kind? And so I asked Him, "Did You do this for
. . . Carmen Benson?"

Tenderly, yet with overpowering majesty, came
His answer. And He didn't just say, "Yes." He said,
"Yes. For Carmen Benson." Jesus called me by
name . . . and that's what broke me!

Such love and compassion streamed down upon
me that it was more than I could bear. I didn't
know anything could affect me so deeply. Bowing
my head, I covered my face with my hands. My
body shook with sobs, and even my hands were
wet with tears.

Instinctively I bent forward until my head
touched the floor. I understood then why Moses
prayed in that position, and why the Bible says
of others: *They fell on their faces and wor-
shipped . . .*

No wonder even "angels prostrate fall" before
the throne and the Lamb. No wonder we sing:

"Crown Him the Lord of Love. Behold
    His hands and side—
  Rich wounds—yet visible above in
    beauty glorified.
No angel in the sky can fully bear that
    sight,
  But downward bends his burning eye
    at mysteries so bright."

The great mystery of the Blood of the Lamb—
we shall never fathom its depths. But for me the
mystery of my vision had been fathomed, and it
was as God had promised. When the answer was
given, I knew it.

The Lord Himself made known the meaning of
the dream's symbols. He who had given the dream
in the first place, was the one who put the pieces
together, and enabled me to understand why He
chose this means of divine intervention:

In the beginning I was part of the milling crowd
that walks this earth. When I was seven years old,
my mother gave me a Bible with the words of
Jesus printed in red ink. These were the only
words I read in that Bible, and I read them over
and over again.

This initial touch of God upon my life as a child
was beautifully represented in the dream by the
pure white bird descending from above and light-
ing on my head. What a fitting symbol of the
Godhead . . . the circle of light, without begin-

ning or end, depicted God the Father; the pure white bird represented Jesus, the Son of God, Who came down from heaven to give His life a ransom for many—including me, personally; the little tongues of fire atop the ring of light graphically depicted the Holy Spirit.

But while I had *believed* in Jesus from those marvelous words I read in the Bible, I had not *received* Him as personal Saviour. He was on my head, not within my heart.

And so, as the years came and went and I walked down the street of life, the lights flickered, and some went out. My childhood belief in Jesus and the Bible dimmed. The focus of my attention was on self and the outer world—the things I had and the things I didn't have that I wanted; my pains and my pleasures; my worries and my fears. I looked around for personality recognition and sense-gratification, the way everyone else I knew did.

Yet there was one sentence from those words printed in red ink that I could not forget, so deeply had it impressed me. This was the sentence:

"For what shall it profit a man, if he shall gain the whole world, and lose his own soul?" (Mark 8:36)

I didn't want to lose my soul. The way to keep from doing this, I decided, was to become a church person; and that is what I did. I even married a church person, just to make sure.

But in time I grew discontent with merely being a church person. Having a genuine desire to grow spiritually, I began to read religious books. Those of the metaphysical variety particularly attracted me. I thought the way to God was through the mind. That was what the church to which I belonged taught, rather than teaching that salvation comes only through the shed blood of Jesus Christ.

I do not put the entire blame on the church for my subsequent entanglement in false religions. I did hear the gospel on the radio. Because of their beautiful music, I listened regularly to several evangelical programs, but I usually turned them off when the preaching commenced.

The gospel I rejected as being "too simple, too easy." How could Jesus die for my sins two thousand years ago, when I hadn't even been born then? And even if such a thing were possible, why should He have to pay for my sins? I should pay for them myself.

That was my opinion, and of course this made me a ready target for many false teachings. When you reject the true gospel as revealed in the Bible, Satan has any number of counterfeit religions available. If you don't fall for one, he has plenty of others to offer.

From the milder metaphysical cults, I "progressed" into Oriental religions and esoteric philosophies, and finally into the occult—and spiritism is about as far away from God as you can get. No wonder the lights in my dream went out!

Yet the living bird never left me. Jesus remained up there in the back of my head somewhere. But eventually, as my understanding became more and more darkened, I felt nothing of my early belief in Him.

Then, through a series of circumstances in my life, I reached the point where I realized I must examine what actually was on top of my head. It was at this moment that I came face to face with my spiritual stumbling block—*Calvary and the blood atonement!* I had been trying to find God by detouring Calvary, and you just can't do it. Christ's shed blood is the only means of salvation; there is no other way.

When I finally saw the truth, I wanted to get rid of all the material I had clothed about myself, and to bring the gospel into the church where I had been deceived and had helped to deceive others.

But they were interested only in the performance of Christianity—the number of people attending, the amount of the offerings, and making the individuals feel important. They did not want the gospel.

"You can't come in here with that!" was indeed the answer of those in authority to the appearance of the gospel in that church. But in my capacity as editor of the weekly publication, I left it there anyway—for as much time as was left. The pastor's new-birth experience soon resulted in his being put out of the church he founded; and I, along with other born-again Christians, left with him.

However, while the church as an organization did not meet my needs, before our expulsion, I found what I was searching for within its walls in a side room. I received the *"washing of regeneration and renewal in the Holy Spirit,"* and became a cleansed worker for God.

The name "Wotan" in the dream was strictly a personal touch the Lord used. To most people it would mean little if anything; but to me—an opera lover—the name had immediate meaning. In Wagnerian operas based on Norse mythology, Wotan—as the chief god—stands for wisdom and victory. It was through that door that I passed; and the abundance of water within this anteroom scripturally symbolizes the blessed Holy Spirit.

Thank God, when we reach the place where we sincerely desire to serve God instead of self, and seek to become as pure and holy as He—there is always a kindly someone who has entered before who is willing to assist us.

Thus ends the story of a strange dream, and the interpretation of it. Was it only a dream?

No . . . It was God's wondrous way of bringing me back to the fold, after I had *"departed from the faith by giving heed to deceitful spirits and doctrines of demons."* The dream, and its interpretation, was the means of my being born again in Christ Jesus.

66

Because of this, I shall still be grateful—even on that bright morning when I awaken . . . in the land where it is always day . . . to dream no more.

TO MY GRANDDAUGHTER

The following is a letter that was written more than a year after the marriage of our daughter, but long before her first pregnancy.

At the time, we had no assurance she could even have a baby. But in my heart there was the certainty that the Lord had a very special baby girl He would be sending, just for us.

Sure enough, a few years later, the baby made an appearance . . . and of course, she was a girl!

You are as yet unborn—a soul waiting somewhere in God's beautiful heaven.

One lovely day you will leave there to come to us here on earth, and an angel will accompany you to the very gateway of human birth. At that moment you will leave that shining kingdom—while into ours you will arrive.

Even now I long to welcome you, to hold you in my arms, to look upon your sweet face, to give you the love that already belongs to you.

For you see, a grandchild is a very special gift. Our children come to us when we are too young to appreciate them fully. Our own lives are just opening up, and we are busy about many things. Parents have a multitude of duties and worries and ambitions that do not weigh so heavily on grandparents.

Then too, grandparents have had a chance to live a little longer, and to learn a little more from life's experiences. Not that we are smarter or know better than your mother and father. It's just that the days of our years have taught us certain things it isn't possible to understand earlier.

Our physical energies have subsided a bit, our emotions are more tranquil, and our ambitions have receded. We do not feel the compelling drive to "get somewhere" in this outer world as once we did. We value things differently, especially the things that really matter.

And so it is that a grandchild comes at just the right time. Youth and vitality and enthusiasm are marvelous and wonderful possessions. Perhaps that's why—when they dim—God grants us a particularly bright and precious gift to replace them.

Oh my little one, child of my child . . . I have so much love to impart to you! So many dreams for you, so much beauty my heart is bursting to share with you.

I want your ears to hear fine music even in your infancy—sacred music, and ethereal melodies from the realm of opera, the incomparable singing that is the glory of the human voice in all its perfection.

Later on I will take you to the ballet, where your eyes will be entranced by the unparalleled grace and exquisite beauty of that form of artistic expression.

We will go for walks in some of the beautiful gardens I have visited, and you will place your trusting little hand in mine. We'll listen to the song of the birds, and feel the soft warm sunshine, and smell the fragrance of grass and trees and flowers.

You will, of course, find your own path of unfoldment in life; but I would have the privilege of showing you the path of beauty. It is strewn with music and harmony and loveliness.

And since the greatest beauty of all is the beauty of holiness, we will talk in quiet moments of God and His goodness. We will thank Him for His love that gave to us His only Son, Jesus Christ our Lord, to be our Saviour. Always, we will say our prayers together when I take care of you.

When you're hungry, I will feed you. When you're tired, we will rest. When you're hurt, I will comfort you. Were it possible, I would shield you forever from all ugliness, all sorrow and sadness, all pain and despair. But that is not within my power or province.

If, occasionally, I am too indulgent with you— or not as strict a disciplinarian as I should be—

may I be pardoned. To me you will be more than a child. You will be the freshness of morning . . . the beginning of springtime . . . the symbol of unbroken dreams . . . the renewal of life and its eternal promise.

In a sense, you will be my own little girl come back again.

All this you will be to me, and I to you . . . for just a little while.

Gradually you will prefer to be with those your own age. That is only natural. I do not expect to have you very much, or for very long, because you came to other arms . . . other hearts . . . other lives than mine.

But for the brief time you will belong to me—for those sweet, innocent years of childhood when your life is like a rose in the bud—though two generations separate us—I will know the companionship of you, the joy of you, the wonder of you.

And when for me a day of departure comes, and an angel of another kind accompanies me through a different gateway . . . may there remain with you—from your grandmother—a spiritual legacy of love and beauty.

THE LONG WAY HOME

In a little Methodist church in Long Beach, California—on a Sunday evening many years ago —a week-long revival meeting was coming to its conclusion.

The last minutes of the last night were ticking away. A final altar call had been given, and the choir was singing ever so softly, *"Just as I am, without one plea, but that Thy blood was shed for me . . . and that Thou bidd'st me come to Thee, O Lamb of God, I come! I come!"*

A few individuals had gone down to the front and were kneeling at the altar rail, one or two in tears. The evangelist left the platform, and still preaching, began to walk up the aisle. He was a big man with a rich, booming voice. His head was crowned with a mass of snow-white hair, and beneath his brows glowed huge penetrating brown eyes.

As he entreated sinners in the congregation to repent and come to Christ, he intently searched the face of every person, row by row. The choir

73

now began to sing, *"Pass me not, O gentle Saviour, hear my humble cry; . . . while on others Thou art calling, do not pass me by."*

Seated in a pew to the evangelist's left, about midway in the church, a fourteen-year-old girl was trembling with fear . . . and I was that girl.

Having joined the church only two weeks before, I didn't feel that God expected me to go down that aisle again. But the sermon had made me very uneasy, for it had clearly named from scripture all those who would NOT inherit the kingdom of God. And at the mention of the word "thieves," my conscience had started to burn.

Once I had stolen a package of Juicy Fruit gum from a dresser drawer in my aunt's home, and had never confessed it to a living soul. The remembrance of this sinful deed had bothered me occasionally, but now it was an active torment. Would it bar me forever from heaven's gate?

The evangelist was slowly approaching my row . . .

I did not dare to meet his searching eyes, for surely guilt must be written all over my face to a man such as he. Lowering my gaze to the floor, I sat in rigid terror. I didn't want the gentle Saviour to pass me by, but how I hoped the evangelist would hurry up and do so!

Desperately I tried to think of other things, to recall the kind look the minister had given me when he received me into the church. He had asked if I believed in Jesus Christ and accepted

Him as my personal Saviour, to which I answered a truthful "Yes." It had always been inconceivable to me that anyone would *not* accept Him. But I had no real understanding of what it meant.

After this "public confession of faith," I was baptized by sprinkling, and a few words were spoken about the forgiveness of sins. At the time I was not conscious of any particular sin, or even of sin in general. All I could think of was how nervous I was; for I had no preliminary instruction or spiritual preparation of any kind.

Now, sitting there fearfully waiting for the evangelist to pass by, I wished I had remembered that gum-stealing episode at the moment of my baptism. If I had, perhaps I wouldn't feel so guilty and ashamed.

Was it possible that I was forgiven anyway?

Yet how could a few drops of water sprinkled on one's head make a person forgiven of anything? It was beyond me . . . But at long last, so also was the evangelist; and I breathed a great sigh of relief.

On the way home that night, I ventured to ask my girl friend's parents a question:

"If you join the church, and confess Jesus, and are baptized, does that mean—no matter what you've done—that you will go to heaven when you die?"

They assured me that this would be true, provided the person continued to lead a Christian life. It seemed to me a very easy way to gain entrance into such a blissful place, but I did not pursue the subject. After all, they had been church people all their lives, and I had not.

My parents were not unbelievers, yet you could hardly call our home a Christian one. Mother occasionally sang a hymn around the house, but we never prayed or went to church.

For a while I attended a Sunday school class for all ages, held in the local grammar school, taught by a Seventh Day Adventist named Mr. Thompson. He was very nice. His wife played the piano, and I learned to sing: *"Jesus wants me for a sunbeam, to shine for Him each day."*

When I was seven years old, my mother gave me a Bible for my birthday. Usually we didn't get anything at all, for money was scarce; so this was indeed a treasured gift. The words of Jesus printed in red ink fascinated me, and I read some of them every day.

I was very proud of that Bible, except for one thing. Printed at the bottom of the title page was the price—fifty cents—which was not objectionable, for it proved my mother had sacrificed to buy it for me. But just above that was the name of the store that sold it—KRESS. I didn't see why that had to be there, and in such large type. I wanted my friends to think my Bible had come from a real book store.

One summer there was a Vacation Bible School in an empty store building in our little community, and I was overjoyed with every minute of it.

When the week was up, I felt sad that such a wonderful week had come to an end.

But the day I shall never forget was the first time I ever went to a real church!

The parents of another girl friend took me with them, and we rode a long way to get there in their new Packard car. Their economic level was far above ours in every way. But the church to which we went completely overwhelmed me with its magnificence.

I was very small for my age then, and I almost lost my balance standing in front of it and looking up trying to see the top of the steeple.

Inside the sanctuary, I was absolutely transfixed by the multicolored stained glass windows, the glorious music, and the vast interior beauty. I never knew anything like this existed! I couldn't imagine heaven itself being any more marvelous than this First Baptist Church of Los Angeles.

With the passing of the years, churchgoing became a regular occurrence; and of course lost much of the glamour with which I had childishly viewed it.

At the age of seventeen I was rebaptized, this time by immersion, when I joined the Wilshire Christian Church. Haunted by a dreadful fear of drowning, I approached the baptismal waters with great emotional suffering. The minister was a small man, and since I was taller than he, I didn't believe he could support me.

Above the baptistry was a large white cross, entwined with Easter lilies, and bathed in a soft pink light. It was the last thing I looked upon before closing my eyes and being submerged.

I thought, "Well, if I'm going to drown, this is a beautiful place to do it."

The only trouble was, I still wasn't sure I was "saved," or good enough, or whatever one had to be, to be confident of going to heaven.

Fright overcame me under the water, and I struggled to get to my feet, reaching out frantically for something to cling to. I didn't want to pull the minister down with me. Just at the most terrifying moment, I felt his strong arm upholding me, and then lifting me up, while he spoke the words, *"Raised—to walk in a new life."*

But again, these were only words whose meaning I was not ready to comprehend.

More than twenty-five years were to follow before I was to be truly baptized—this time washed with my own tears, and plunged in the sweet depths of the crystal fountain of Christ's love. And this time my mind was not on myself, but where it belonged—on Him, into Whom I was baptized . . .

But oh the searching of those twenty-five years! Twenty-five years of faithful church attendance, working in the Sunday school and with young people, in the women's organizations, and as an employee on the staff of the church. Years during which I read a multitude of spiritual books, filling notebooks with their excerpts. Years in which I studied all the religions of the world, attending lectures and classes, becoming particularly well informed in the metaphysical sciences. Years in which I prayed frequently and spent time in meditation. I even read the Bible . . .

A quarter of a century in the church, but not in Christ.

I was an earnest "truth seeker." I followed this teaching and that, searched here and searched there. I found much intellectual stimulation, some helpful psychology, many interesting people. But I did not find the answer to the deep-seated need of my soul. I did not find Him, Who Himself *is* the Truth.

No one finds Him in the mind alone; He must be found through the heart. Even when we prove God's existence through logic and reason, until we are ready to receive Jesus Christ in the heart, He will continue to elude us.

Yet we can become so absorbed in our religious activity—be it intellectual or organizational—and so comfortable in our churchianity and self-approval that we think we are sailing the high seas of the spirit, bound for the heavenly harbor. And all the while we aren't even on the boat! Worse still, we don't even know that we've missed it!

The average Christian, the good church person like me, takes it for granted that he is in the kingdom. Jesus, however, very plainly said, *"Unless you are born again, you cannot see the kingdom* of God." We cannot even *see* it, let alone enter it!

And Jesus also said, *"Except you be converted, and become as little children, you shall not enter into the kingdom of heaven."* To be converted from *self*—that is the hard part!

I—who had mentally looked down on others, thinking I knew so much more than they—actually knew nothing. Because with all my knowledge of religions and philosophies, I did not know the Lord. Just knowing about Him, or just assuming we know Him, doesn't make it so. When we once have a real, vital, personal, living encounter and experience with Him, we *know* we know Him from that day on. And like Saint Paul, we count everything else as nothing for the surpassing worth of knowing Christ Jesus, the Lord.

When at last I found Him for myself, it happened in the old-fashioned way—on my knees in deep prayer; not at an altar rail, but alone with Him in my own home. Alone, at the foot of His cross—when God in His wisdom let me see the meaning of a dream He'd given me. And when I came to Him in true repentance, there was a lot more than a stolen package of Juicy Fruit gum on my conscience.

But all the stains of all the years were washed away forever in His precious blood. And at long last, I fully understood what forgiveness of sins really means, and from whence it comes.

True, indeed, were the words the choir had sung so long ago:

"Just as I am—Thou wilt receive,
Wilt welcome, pardon, cleanse, relieve;
Because Thy promise I believe,
O Lamb of God, I come! I come!"

Wonderful as it is, being born anew is just the beginning. There is the life of the Spirit to be lived—a growing up in Christ to do—the joy and richness of becoming more deeply and intimately acquainted with Him. Each day becomes a brand new opportunity to get to know Him better, to understand His teaching more clearly.

Before long, I discovered a strange thing. Changes were taking place in me. I was different. *"For if any man is in Christ, he is a new creature. Old things are passed away; behold all things are become new."*

For one thing, I was reading and studying the Bible every possible moment and hour of the day and night that I could devote to it. I was like a famished person at a banquet table, and the words of Jesus were food and drink to my hungry soul.

Chapters that I had read before, as one would read a history book, were now like a love letter just arrived in the morning mail. I could hardly wait to get my work done so I could get to the Bible.

I played sacred music on my radio at home and in the car. I listened to religious programs, one after another . . . *really listened* to every spoken word, and to every word of the music. I wanted to think and talk about spiritual truths all the time.

Often in the night or early morning I would wake up and realize Someone had been talking to me while I slept, teaching me, opening up the Scriptures and bringing to my remembrance many things.

Other times I would wake up singing or humming the words of an old hymn. I felt a kinship with all those song writers who had known the love of Jesus and had expressed it in so many beautiful and melodic ways.

No wonder they called Him the Rose of Sharon, the Lily of the Valley, the Bright Morning Star, the Fairest of Ten Thousand, Precious Lord, Beautiful Saviour, Blest Redeemer, Wonderful Friend . . . ! Now I knew why.

For I too was in love—in love with the Lover of my soul. And wonder of wonders—He loved me in return! He loved me for myself—not for anything I had or could give Him or do for Him. Not like any earthly love, but with a pure unbounded love divine.

I wanted to learn more of Him, to serve Him, to do His will, to be what He would have me be. In addition to my regular prayer time, half-a-dozen times a day at odd intervals I would drop to my knees just to tell Him I loved Him, and to thank Him for His loving kindness.

I wanted to tell others, "There's no one like Him! All you can ever desire is to be found in

Him. He heals every heartache, calms every fear, strengthens, companions, guides you safely through this world of trials and tribulation."

Gradually I became aware that He was not only *with* me, but *in* me. I was living, yet Someone else—or something else that had never been there before—was dwelling in my mind and heart.

This Someone was better than anything I had ever been, or ever could become on my own. This Someone was all good—not a mixture of good and bad, like me. This One was compassionate toward others, not critical like me. Selfless, not selfish like me. Always serene and peaceful, full of faith and trust—not anxious and nervous like me. This Someone was wise, with a wisdom as ancient as time.

Was this the Holy Spirit—the Comforter, the Spirit of Truth, the Blessed Third Person of the Trinity—Whom the dear Lord had promised to send? How could these things be? I was not worthy of such a gift. What could I ever do to repay Him for all that He had done for me?

Today, no trace remains of the teenager of long ago who had been so uncertain about heaven. I could drown tomorrow—in a baptistry or out of it—and I would fear no evil. For in my heart is the blessed assurance that when I am absent from the body, I will be at home with the Lord.

At home with Him! How wonderful!

Longingly, I think about the place that He said He had gone to prepare for those who love Him. That's where I want to be, with Him in His kingdom. And that's where I shall be, for He has promised me a place among those who are sanctified by faith in Him.

How marvelous of God to provide a Way whereby we can be transformed from our human self-centeredness and sinfulness and ignorance into Christ's glorious life! Transformed step by step into His likeness.

If we love Him and keep His Word, He does abide in us and we in Him. And we will grow in spiritual maturity, until at last He is able to present us without a blemish before the presence of God, clad in the robes of His own righteousness.

And there in that holy city we shall know no more sickness, pain, sorrow or tears; no more old age or death; no more parting; no more ugliness or darkness. And all whose names are written in the Lamb's Book of Life shall worship Him, and shall see His face, and be with Him forevermore . . .

Yes, it was the long way home for me, since that Sunday evening in the little Methodist church of years ago. And in retrospect, perhaps it does appear an unforgivable sin to have lived so near something—something so beautiful and so splendid as the Lord Jesus Christ—and not have recognized Him.

But when at last my eyes beheld the King in His beauty, and the highlands of heaven far away —like the debtor of old to whom He forgave the most, I love Him more because of it.

Suggested Inspirational Paperback Books

FACE UP WITH A MIRACLE
  —by Don Basham $1.25
    This is a fascinating book about God
    the Holy Spirit bringing a new dimen-
    sion into the lives of twentieth-century
    Christians. It is filled with experiences
    that testify to a God of miracles being
    unleashed in our lives right now.

BAPTISM IN THE HOLY SPIRIT: COMMAND
  OR OPTION?—by Bob Campbell $1.25
    A teaching summary on the Holy
    Spirit, covering the three kinds of bap-
    tisms, the various workings of the Holy
    Spirit, the question of tongues and how
    to know when you have received the
    Baptism of the Spirit.

A SCRIPTURAL OUTLINE OF THE BAPTISM IN
  THE HOLY SPIRIT
  —by George and Harriet Gillies   50¢
    Here is a very brief and simple outline
    of the Baptism in the Holy Spirit, with
    numerous references under each point.

This handy little booklet is a good reference for any question you might have concerning this subject.

A HANDBOOK ON HOLY SPIRIT BAPTISM
—by Don Basham $1.25
Questions and answers on the Baptism in the Holy Spirit and speaking in tongues. The book is in great demand, and answers many important questions from within the contemporary Christian Church.

HE SPOKE, AND I WAS STRENGTHENED
—by Dick Mills $1.25
An easy-to-read devotional of 52 prophetic scripturally-based messages directed to the businessman, the perfectionist, the bereaved, the lonely, the ambitious and many more.

SEVEN TIMES AROUND
—by Bob and Ruth McKee $1.25
A Christian growth story of a family who receives the Baptism in the Holy Spirit and then applies this new experience to solve the family's distressing, but frequently humorous problems.

LET GO!—by Fenelon   95¢
Jesus promised a life full of joy and peace. Why then are so many Chris-

tians struggling to attain the qualities
that Christ said belonged to the child
of God? Fenelon speaks firmly—but
lovingly to those whose lives have
been an uphill battle. Don't miss this
one.

VISIONS BEYOND THE VEIL—by H. A. Baker   95¢
Beggar children who heard the gospel
at a rescue mission in China, received
a powerful visitation of the Holy
Spirit, during which they saw visions
of heaven and Christ which cannot be
explained away. A new revised edition.

DEAR DAD, THIS IS TO ANNOUNCE MY
DEATH—by Ric Kast $1.25
The story of how rock music, drugs
and alcohol lead a youth to commit
suicide. While Ric waits out the last
moments of life, Jesus Christ rescues
him from death and gives him a new
life.

GATEWAY TO POWER—by Wesley Smith $1.25
From the boredom of day after day
routine and lonely nights of meaning-
less activity, Wes Smith was caught
up into a life of miracles. Dramatic
healings, remarkable financial assist-
ance, and exciting escapes from dan-
gerous situations have become part of
his life.

SIGI AND I—by Gwen Schmidt   95¢
> The intriguing narration of how two
> women smuggled Bibles and supplies
> to Christians behind the Iron Curtain.
> An impressive account of their simple
> faith in following the Holy Spirit.

MINISTERING THE BAPTISM IN THE HOLY
SPIRIT—by Don Basham $1.00
> Over 100 received their Baptism after
> hearing the author give this important
> message. The book deals with such
> topics as the Baptism as a second ex-
> perience, the primary evidence of the
> Baptism, and tongues and the "Chronic
> Seeker."

THE LAST CHAPTER—by A. W. Rasmussen $1.25
> An absorbing narrative based on the
> author's own experience, in the charis-
> matic renewal around the world. He
> presents many fresh insights on fasting,
> church discipline and Christ's Second
> Coming.

A HANDBOOK ON TONGUES, INTERPRETATION
AND PROPHECY—by Don Basham $1.25
> The second of Don Basham's Hand-
> book series. Again set up in the con-
> venient question and answer format,
> the book addresses itself to further
> questions on the Holy Spirit, especially
> the vocal gifts.

12-74